MAD RIVER

MAD RIVER

poems by Justin Bigos

GOLD WAKE

Contents

*

for Erin

Prayer (After Refusing to Pray)

Now, in the summer heat of Texas
in February, to the sound of grackles
in trees stretching for rain, I pray
for a man over a thousand miles
away. But You—if You are
what he says You are—have
sent boys to burn the car
that was his home, boys
to crack his skull with stones,
and now You send a boy to drag him
down to a river dark with snow
and push him in. Water
in his mouth, his eyes—did he
think of me? But it was
the ocean I'd found myself
inside. I had refused to pray
all summer, and when I emerged
from the salty sting of blindness,
my body dripping with the Atlantic,
I refused again, and my father wept.
And You—or so a boy thinks—
did not lift a finger.
Come, You in Your silver suit
of water, spread Your
length across these rocky plains.
Turn those eyes large as whales
to what my only father,
barely breathing on his back,
calls the heavens—tell me
what it is You see.

Twenty Thousand Pigeons

In my dream last night, back again on the corner
of Avenue J and 14th, a rabbinical student stops me

to ask if I'm Jewish. I show him the framed photo
I carry: a family of nine. Pale faces, strong noses; black hair

parted or pulled back; the children dressed like the parents.
He says, They, are they Jewish? I don't know, I say.

In my dream last night, Hungaria. The baker of small rolls
says, Can I help you? He means, Are you Jewish?

A loaf of rye, I say. He looks behind him, racks and racks
of loaves, buns, bagels, twists. We have something that is not rye?

he says. And, Why are you saying Hungaria,
Mr. America? I take the steamship to Prague

and all the statues salute me. The young women blow out
kisses like candles, their hair wheat against the scythes

of their cheekbones. No one will let me finish saying,
Will you marry me, or Please, only a sip of your blackberry brandy.

In my dream, the twenty thousand pigeons killed in the war
rise thunderous as waterfalls, and so I walk the suspension bridge

from Austria to Niagara and my father and his father
and the crowd of fathers behind them

greet me with a simple pair of shoes, a jar of herring in dill,
a Cherokee headdress, one black potato, a wine glass

to crush under which foot they will not say.

My Father's Car

Because it is winter, scrape
the frost off the rear window
to see the styrofoam cup

spilling nickels and dimes.
Notice that the backseat
has been ripped out

to make room for the one-eyed cat.
You can see the leather biker's hat
over my father's face

and his barrel chest rise and fall
like the metal ball that measures
the force of a carnival hammer.

Squint at his briefcase—
it sits in the passenger seat, half-open;
the corner of an eviction notice.

The Bible on the dashboard,
all the bookmarks in Revelation.
Put an ear to the roof

and hear my father murmur
about cancer, the lottery, and how the demons
tap the hubcaps with their ballpoint pens.

Don't bother scanning
for whiskey bottles, cigarettes,
or any vice you can hold in your hand.

If you stand back from this car
and take the loupe from your eye,
you will be forced to admit

there is such a thing as bad luck.
This is my father's home.
Take it in your hands and gently shake.

The Superintendent

The air as still as bathwater, no breeze
from Sheepshead, we carry clear plastic bags
of empty bottles and cans, blue plastic bags
of plastic bottles and milk jugs, we squeeze
flattened boxes into open boxes, then tie
it all in twine—but do we cover it
in tarp in case it rains? He says, *Forget-
about-it*, just like on TV. (I'd died
a little when he asked me for my help
after mumbling something about the blacks
and Jews, this man who once refused to attack
his neighbors in Croatia, then fled that hell
—I've heard it said—with three-thousand cash
inside his socks.) And next we do the trash.

Three Rooftops

It happens on rooftops: the jump, the cut, the kiss smack between
	the stripper's
breasts, your lover holding her lips right there, watching you
	watch.

October, 2001, Chinatown highrise apartment building, flags of
	restaurants and America
whipping below, before the sordid and banal became
	photographed

on phones, dilated cyclopean eyes, sent to other eyes across the
	globe, across the room,
the rooftop. Now she's dancing with some guy, some dude, tall
	and lanky like you

but embarrassingly determined. You like watching this, knowing
	you're the only one who gets
to take her to bed, 3 a.m. or 5:49 a.m., cab up to Amsterdam and
	106th,

the stumbling up the stairs, fumbling with the keys, the jeans,
	shoulders and tongues
loosening, and while she grins and shakes her ass for this dude,

you remember the question Gina from Indiana just asked: How
	long have you lived here?
She is soap-commercial pretty and she's tweezed

the shit out of her eyebrows, so you think of Ingrid Bergman in
	Vertigo
and how her stunt double fell down all those stairs to a cold

cushion in Hollywood. And your lover, years ago in Rome, a
        teenager fooling around
with a semi-pro soccer player, Marco or Fabrizio, the most
        beautiful legs

she'd ever seen, and you wonder how any woman could French
        kiss a grown man
wearing shorts. But, of course, he goes for her tits. He's Italian

and wearing a crucifix and then he sees it: the mezuzah hanging on
        a chain
from her neck. She's told you what happens next: the street below
        rushing

toward her, thinking she would die as he held her over the edge of
        the rooftop
and called her Jew, the word itself a slur, and how he made one
        slow incision

in her chest with the pendant. Rome, which gave us a colosseum
        built by twenty thousand
Jewish slaves, *ossobuco, gelato,* and the *ghetto.*

She's dancing now with her friend J., and you've always liked to
        watch two female friends
dance, the undeniable flirting, the mirrored affection,

how they never take their eyes off each other. All in the eyes.
        Remember? Pittsburgh,
the 1990s, two men in the corner of an overcrowded drug party,

both coked up and one leaning in and asking the other if he wants
        to do some E, and maybe
get blown? The eyes: tired, begging. The other eyes: *I'm sorry.*

And so a few hazy moments later, while a man and woman sit and
		share a first kiss
on a drizzly rooftop, the jilted man who did take E walks out to

the edge and steps off. The couple sees it from the corner of half-
		lidded eyes.
They had just figured out something about each other

and now the ambulance lights and the young man's friend, look at
		the eyes, he's in love,
saying how many fingers, what year is it, saying who's the
		president

name your favorite movie just keep your eyes open, crying over
		his bloody friend.
Who lives, it turns out, and suffers not a single broken bone,

his body deliciously slack from the drugs. You could tell Gina this
		story,
say something like, Passing out half-dressed with a friend you've
		fucked

for the first time after some kid jumps off a roof is the crowning
		achievement
of Western Civilization, but you say, Just a few months.

She wants to say something about September 11th but doesn't. The
		eyes: intelligent,
confused. Gina from Indiana could take you to some all-night

dim sum joint and toy purposefully with an earring, but it wasn't
		Ingrid Bergman,
was it? It was Kim Novak. With eyes like your lover's,

though hazel instead of blue, an impostor, hiding at the top of the
		bell tower
while her evil lover pushed the body of his dead wife

from one of the tower's windows. No rooftop to speak of, just a
    room at the top
with a church bell. Then the nun ringing it after Novak

does, in the end, fall. The dude and your lover, your best friend,
    are at it again,
and her eyes tell you, I'm so bored, okay, you win, and I win

too, take me home. No shenanigans in the cab, just her head on
    your shoulder,
clichéd and comfortable. The taxi ferries you up the island, block
    after block

of bright and empty windows. She falls asleep. Then wakes, eyes
    closed,
her muskmelon breath whispering your common, forgettable
    name.

Portrait of My Mother with Food Stamps

In high heels and bruised peach
eyeshadow, in the check-out
lane for twelve items or less,

she thumbs through the wad
like a Rolodex of ex-lovers
on a lonely Friday night,

one acrylic, candy-apple-
red nail scraping blue,
green, yellow bills like those

I hoard at home for Boardwalk
and Park Place, my little metal
choo-choo train coming around

the corner of the jail. Time
is sweet, and that's how my mother
takes hers, extra cream and sugar

in the smile; the cashier, sucking
her top teeth, repeats the gaudy
tally: *One-hundred-eighty-six*

and 12 cent. In black rabbit fur
down to her calves, amethyst
earrings jacketed in gold—

all stolen by her new man—
this white woman, my mother,
is so ashamed to be here

she's going to flaunt it. *Hundred
eighty-six* dollars, she says,
and twelve cents. *Thank you,*

*ma'am. Thank you, President
Reagan*, and even the customers
behind us can't help but chuckle.

But my mother's not laughing.
She's counting and recounting
the colorful bills we waited

two hours for this morning
in a line snaking around
a city block, the whole world,

she'd said, breathing
down our backs. She winks.
Throws down 190 in stamps.

Says, *Keep the change.*

Photograph of My Stepfather with Handguns

From the waist up, in black and white,
he is a free man. Arms raised
in mock pat-down, loaded holster
under each shoulder. He wears a face
shaved clean, mouth caught
between laugh and sneer.
Crucifix on a chain; three buttons
undone. Pomade, pinky ring,
and suspenders. It's '50s gangster
without the fedora, without
the blood. Whoever shot this
only pressed a button:
this is self-portrait
in the come-and-get-it style
of a man I never met.

In the gravel of I-95 with a shredded tire,
my stepfather looks at the photo, pulpy and creased
in my hand. *I used to be a stick-up guy,* he says.
That's it. He doesn't know I know: the time
in jail, three felonies, numbers rackets
and hijacked trucks, the bullets
in his back. I've seen the scars clustered
around his spine; how his body moves
only when it needs to, like the Boss
he never was. My mother warned me
not to ask questions. An accident, maybe,
this photo stashed in the glove compartment
with a flashlight—or an old charm
against those who'd dare to stop him running
red lights. He slams the door.
I get on the ground. I keep my mouth shut.
I work quickly in the dark
with the little light he gives me.

Fassbinder

He couldn't wait to finish a film before
he started the next, forty-three total plus
the nine-hundred-thirty-minute TV series;
refused to commit to any one lover,
man or woman; fucked his actors in Munich
hotels and Morocco chateaus; left a trail
of broken hearts, one ex-wife, four wrecked
Lamborghinis, two suicides; popped pills
to stay awake and pills to fall asleep,
coke, booze, you name it; lit one cigarette
off another, ate the worst German
foods, braunschweiger and bratwurst
fried in fat, had to get it all down, squeeze
it all in and keep it up, never enough
time, the work the work was all that mattered
it was never enough, I'm saying
out of breath at 2:47 a.m. to
the woman I want to marry

Oración por Tim Cook

A shorn male Medusa,
he sauntered through alleys
swinging time on a chain.
His eyes were frozen mudslides.
His nose a first fight.
Teeth fish-hooked minnows.
Laugh a music box
spilling stolen necklaces.
He once took a woman in $600
worth of lingerie to an abandoned freight car
beside the French Broad River,
his tongue hot ice
on her lavender nipples.
He once resuscitated Zelda Fitzgerald
from her sanctuary of flame
and made her dance, dance,
dance her life away.
He was a time warp,
a switch of the blade, a tear in the denim,
a thirty-one-year-old teenager
in love. He was the unpaid
tour guide of our hearts.
Where has he gone?
To the bottom of Snake Lake,
where Poseidon and St. Patrick
flay themselves in eternal apologia.
We pray for Tim Cook,
for his limbs to break,
for his skull to crack,
for his beloved serpents to feed
on the stony remains of their king. Amen.

St. Patrick's Day, Chicago

*By 1900, civil engineers had reversed the flow of the
Chicago River.*

Broken river, you're not broken after all.
Raw sewage lake, you're fathomed like an ocean.
We've turned you green and puke green,
respectively, but it's we who envy you.
After how many years does running in
the wrong direction become, if not right,
at least something people stop noticing,
as they walk the bridge, walk their dogs
dressed like Pekingese Celtophiles? Chicago,
you were not my first choice of anything,
but the woman I followed here had better ideas
than to live in a place called Missouri. Yes,
misery. Misery loves coffee. And sunflower
seeds and bus passes. And a stranger on a bench
with a braid in a braid, her un-ringed finger
stuck in a wedding magazine. And misery loves
her dog, barking at a cloud which is a sky.

Patron Saint,

who do you watch over tonight, the lovers in the alleys
of Chicago, its one river running backward for over a hundred
years, dyed green, Patron Saint of Roberta Flack, blue lights
in the basement, another cigarette lit but here comes
the first kiss, again, how many times can you have a first kiss,
Patron Saint, it's a silly and a sad question, tongue on the teeth
and yes, this is how she smells, cherrywood and armpits,
which never get enough love, I mean both literally and figuratively,
you armpit licker extraordinaire, you toenail biter, Patron Saint
of flip flops on the dashboard, sundress creeping up the thighs,
some early nasal Dylan on the FM, Patron Saint of the static
and Spanish and Haitian at the end of the dial, getting a little
turned on in the driver's side, it's okay, Patron Saint, me too,
memory as hot as the vinyl seats in the Pontiac or, screw
memory, let's go with a Corvette, Patron Saint of stolen cars
and junk shops, tow trucks and cinderblocks, ratchet wrenches,
coffee burnt, what other liquid do we call burnt, scorched milk,
boiled water, but coffee we say is burnt, the floor needs swept
in Pittsburgh, where the soder is pop and the bologna is jumbo
and we're goin' donton to watch the Stillers, O Patron Saint
are you even watching the game, do you watch over the teams
named for industry, Packers and 49ers and Pistons, the jackhammer-
ing of America, but let's not be nationalists, Patron Saint, too late
for that, just ask Greece, ask Cavafy, it's always the same city,
the city inside the city, the river under the river, clothesline
reaching from my window to your window, Brooklyn 2003
or Palermo 1956, it doesn't matter anymore, Patron Saint of bloody
cranesbill, foxglove, cattail, plants named for animals, and animals,
well, why don't we name them for plants, an Eastern Himalayan
broad leaf, for example, could be a bird, sounds better than tragopan
in my opinion, Patron Saint, and don't feather and leaf come
from the same – what, what would you call it, Patron Saint, what
is it in particular that you have been assigned, I just read something
about butt sex that makes the rectum bloom into what apparently

is called a rosebud, let's not dwell on it too long, to each his or her
or their own asshole, Patron Saint of fart jokes, of banana jokes,
of Krapp's last tape spoooooooooooling and unspooling, spittle
on the beard, eyes glazed as donuts, someone had to say it, *Be*
        again,
be again, all that old misery, once wasn't enough for you ...
Patron Saint, can you hear me, I'm speaking through the holes
in the plexiglass, I'm putting my hands up so you can wand me,
do you like that verb, to wand, Patron Saint of neon logisms,
HO--- DEPOT, -ELF STORAGE, S----UCKS COFFEE,
--NASTY BUFFET, Patron Saint of splinters on the chopsticks,
as fine as caterpillar hair but there they are, just rub them
together, Patron Saint, I mean the chopsticks not the caterpillars,
not the legs of crickets, they got it, they're good, it's what
they were made for, if you believe in Creation, that is,
Patron Saint, am I losing you, are you keeping your eye on
something else, homie, can I call you homie, paisano, vato,
Big Bro, it's 2014, Patron Saint, are you getting fungry, as the kids
say, it means fucking hungry, O Pastry Chef, Patrón shot
with lime, the father shot once in the back of the head
on the warped docks of Long Island Sound, Patron Saint
of longshoreman handing out union literature amongst workers
but also the goombahs, Patron Saint of bigos bubbling
on the stove, yes it's my name but also a Polish pork stew,
Patron Saint, have we reached the one small thing you stand
watch over, a pork stew simmering for days in its own cabbage
juices and herbs and you can even add dried apricots
and nuts, it's a hunter's stew made to provide sustenance
for days, weeks, you can keep adding meat to it, Patron Saint,
you add sliced apple, you can keep transforming it day
after day after day, but each day is seamed by night, or
is it the other way around, Patron Saint of oiled hinges
and elbow crooks, the backs of knees, the buckling
and unbuckling of dungarees, that's what he called them,
my father, my father who art in every poem I write,
the secret whatever Ginsberg called Cassady, the litany
itself, though not, Patron Saint, the Patron Saint

that is you, we need a third presence even though my dad
hated Catholicism, we need a third because now it's just
you and me, Patron Saint, any old song will do,
some Roberta Flack on vinyl, let's bring her back,
the closer I get to you, the more you make me see,
Patron Saint, let's do it the other way around, I'm feeling
generous, here are my old love letters, my first kiss
that tasted like frost on a windowpane, here is a jar
filled with herring and dill and sour cream, I don't mean
to overwhelm you with this world, Patron Saint,
just take one of these things, and watch over it, nothing
in this world is ours, you know that, you need me
like I need you, this crocodile fern, and some sun.

Empire

This morning, our first snow.
It only sticks to roofs,

the grass still green and brown.
Right now we are bombing Baghdad.

I've finished my coffee, lit another
cigarette. The halogen-white ceiling,

the windows fogging up. Neighbors
leaving for work and coming home

from work. In the kitchen, bacon popping.
Right now my father sleeps somewhere

in Connecticut, in a car, the wind-
shield shattered, tires slashed.

The flurries rushing up, lingering
down, blowing right, left, right.

This morning I sit in an overstuffed chair,
the thermostat steady at seventy-two.

Pittsburgh, 1998

Three Rivers

The whole house is gone, burned in rainy Pittsburgh,
where I used to sit wrapping sticky rice in nori,
drinking whiskey, waiting for you and him to come

stumbling up the stairs, your body folded over
his thick shoulder—laughing, asleep, crying. My days
depended on which. I'd stay seated at the window;

on the table phyllo under a damp paper towel,
porcini mushrooms in a bowl, a plastic pastry brush,
a sauce pan of clarified butter; four strips

of dough, skin-thin, spaced an inch apart,
dressed with brush, layered, dressed with brush,
layered and dressed twice more, the table shaking

each time the train steamed along beneath it,
each time that felt like forever. This morning, forgive me,
I saw you on the blue wing of a raven.

Here, in the mountains of Arizona, the jays
look shellacked, tar-stiff crests, black beaks and eyes
polished by cinder. This is alpine desert, and it smokes

at the slightest touch of water. I have cooked this summer
at the one white tablecloth restaurant for forty miles.
Each night I clock out I hold up my apron—always

a new action-painting of demi-glace, butter and oil, blood
already browned. No pattern, no theme, no face emerging
at last with merciful news—just a pitch-thick

stain, something to be boiled and bleached, scrubbed out
with both hands. I won't ask how you did it.
Won't ask your husband if the police lifted, carried

your body before he could, or if he could have, given
the chance. How the two planes must have lifted
from the ground of Rochester, New York, at different times

but on the same path, to take each of you back
to Pittsburgh, to bury you where you were born.
Forgive me. All I want is to remember you

alive, to wake you from the couch where one night
you lay beside me, blind with alcohol, your breath
somehow sweet. I remember leaving you there

to wander the streets, the alleys, the hollow
below the streets and alleys, then along the bank
of the Allegheny, one of two rivers entering the mouth

of a third, the Ohio, deep and wide and a blue so close
to black if not for the moon, behind the clouds,
the rain. And I thought of you, him, the short days

under one roof, and how, some nights, winter reaches
the point of freezing the mind, like a block of ice
in a river that tries to warm the ice, but can only

make it, for a little while, a little less cold.
But I did not think any of that. No, I didn't wander
the streets of a rainy city with the sole wish of being

swallowed whole. I simply went outside
for a cigarette, and stared up at our dark windows,
then down at the train tracks below the bridge.

It might have been ten minutes. Or less than a moment,
a pulse. Or I stood there for twelve years.
And now, when I turn back toward the house?

My dear, the whole thing is on fire, it is
fire, burning itself from the inside out, a furnace,
a ravenous blindness. And when I look again:

sunrise on glass.

Mad River

They kept saying leave nothing out, I can still hear them saying
leave nothing out while I went on talking without a break
about the incident in the parking lot behind 7-Eleven. Not really
a parking lot, not the main one anyway, but a lot
behind that lot, behind the store, where clerks unloaded
palettes, broke down boxes, smoked cigarettes, weed and, yeah,
I remember, parked their own busted-up cars. So it was a lot,
sort of, and next door: something #5. Not right next door,
but a little down the hill, to the left, if you are in the main lot
for customers, facing the 7-Eleven, to the left
maybe thirty-five or forty yards, like a good breakaway
run by a halfback, not half the length of a football field—but close,
China Palace, no, China Garden, China Garden #5.
They had cats by the dumpster, at least two litters,
coon cats and dirty tabbies, mackerels and spotteds,
and some of the clerks said they, the Chinese, fed those cats
so they could feed them to the customers, call it duck or chicken,
sweet and sour, stay or to go. Really, just one clerk said so: Jimmy.
Jimmy, I'll get to Jimmy. But behind that lot, and behind the lot
of 7-Eleven, behind all the other lots of our little town,
of the laundromat and package store and the boarded-up
Italian bakery, there was a drop-off, a little cliff, a kind of ledge,
something you could stand at the edge of or even lie down on,

your elbows right on the lip of the precipice, and stare out.
Or down, into the Mad River, flowing underneath the town lights
and the sky at night like that thought you'd thought you'd buried.
That's where I pushed him. Where I shoved him, after I hit him.
Sucker-punched him, to be fair. With my right fist, though
I'm left-handed. I never understood that part, even when they said
leave nothing out, nothing, I said I struck him with my right fist,
but the fact is I'm left-handed. The fact is: he would have drowned,
without me.
          I have to walk in order to think,
I've always been this way, I told them, since that seemed important,
me needing to walk in order to think, and not just about the
      incident
but also about my girlfriend, school, my grades, very good
that year, all A's and one B, in art, an elective my senior year,
a nagging interest, something to not have to think about too much,
or if you are walking and thinking about something else, there it is,
the sudden and strange thought: I would like to try my hand
at painting, or college is not for me, or I would like to kiss Abby
who is not my girlfriend, and I hate the Beatles and all my parents'
music and I will tear the "Imagine" poster off my wall soon
as I get home. It seems like you should get an A in something
that won't hurt anyone. I told them this, and even though they said
leave nothing out I knew they would soon have my report cards,
my one speeding ticket, my karate trophies and condoms,

my journal I had stopped writing in for no reason

in the third grade. But I'd kept the journal. I told them this

but they said get back to the incident. We were inside

a small room, not as I'd imagined it, an office like my father's,

a few university degrees and photos framed on the wall,

a coat rack, a desk lamp with a gold chain, green sheath.

The sergeant sat next to me, instead of behind the desk,

so that when I tried to say everything I could remember

it felt like an invisible judge was in the chair behind the desk,

and the sergeant, sitting beside me, talking direct, yet soft,

full eye contact, his knees touching mine, once or twice

brushing me in his pleated navy police pants, deferring

to this unseen presence, this absence, questioning and transcribing,

doing his duty on a yellow legal pad almost out of paper,

there were maybe three or four sheets left as he was writing

      quickly,

leaving nothing out, the pad bending a little as he wrote,

as he pressed the Bic pen into paper, and I wondered

what would happen when he got to that last yellow sheet,

when he got to the bottom of it, a phrase he in fact said,

when they'd d brought me in, uncuffed, I wasn't sure why,

they wanted to get to the bottom of it and so I should

leave nothing out, what would happen then?—the last sheet

flipped and the legal pad bare, just a flimsy piece of cardboard,

the burgundy chair behind the desk tall and empty and oiled

in the dim light.

And so I walked in my mind, I mean in my mind
I walked, in order to think, but I did not walk behind the 7-Eleven,
or anywhere along the embankment, the ridge, nowhere near
the Mad River, but instead in my mind I walked around Nig's Pond,
a horrible name, I knew, I know, it wasn't until junior high
that I understood why, the pond called Cumberland Pond
until the early '70s, when a black boy drowned there,
in the pond, no suspects, an innocent drowning, so they said,
they say even today, though no witnesses, no investigation,
no coroner or D.A., the boy's parents and sisters moving away,
just days after the wake, though some say there was no funeral,
not in this town, anyway. I walked around and around and around
Nig's Pond, which I still call by that name, if only in my head,
to be honest, to not look away, to leave nothing out and in fact
that is where I met the man I later struck. The preacher man,
the people in the town called him, those who called him anything.
Most called him nothing, as if he weren't there, though he was,
had been for years, decades, no one seemed to know his family,
his age, not even his Christian name, the preacher man.
He wore dark denim jeans and a jacket, a suit jacket, I mean,
and he carried a briefcase in one hand and a Bible in
the other, under the arm, the right one, I believe, the Bible,
and maybe that's why he said, I heard him say, though he was
talking

34

only to himself, as he walked around and around Nig's Pond

he said don't let your right hand know what your left hand is doing,

or was it, is it, the other way around, it's from the Bible,

I know, and the preacher man carried the Bible under

his right arm, tucked into his armpit, I do remember,

but was he saying to not let the Bible know what the briefcase

was doing, or had he gotten it backward, gotten it wrong,

was it don't let the briefcase know what the Bible was doing,

what important documents did the preacher man carry,

what old photos of family, what passages bookmarked

in scripture, for when he sat down, the one time he sat down

on one of two benches on the gravel path that circles

Nig's Pond, one bench facing the other at the tips,

the narrowest parts of the pond, for it's an oval, not a circle,

he sat on one bench and I sat on the other, and to pretend

I wasn't watching him I looked at my watch, almost midnight,

11:58 p.m. I'd taken a walk to think, not a habit

newly formed but unexamined, as the preacher man began

to rifle through his Bible, he sat on the bench directly

opposite mine, facing me, except that his face was in the Bible,

he was looking for something, I could see he had dog-eared

and bookmarked various passages of scripture, his favorites

or maybe his least favorites, those passages that tormented him,

that kept him awake at night so that he must reckon with them,

but he couldn't find what he was looking for, and he mumbled, he muttered, he stammered, I was too far away to hear the words,

maybe fifty-five or sixty yards, but I could hear the struggle,

across the pond, not an echo, for there was nothing to echo off

except me: not substantial enough, too thin, not having eaten

for days, no, the sound carried like bird calls across the pond,

across the water, I don't know the name, echolocation

maybe, though that may not be the sound but rather the detection

of the sound, by birds, or bats, circling in the air, in the dark,

and the preacher man had stood, I hadn't noticed, and he was

    circling,

or ovaling, we could call it ovaling, to be exact,

he'd resumed his ovaling of Nig's Pond, and instead of rising

I kept my seat, I don't know why, and in four or five minutes

he was passing me, as if I weren't there at all, an empty bench

he passed, briefcase in one hand, Bible in the other,

not in the armpit but now at the hip, his work boots, I noticed

he was wearing Timberland boots, caked with dirt, saying

to not let one hand know what the other is doing.

                                   Do not walk awa

early enough and it is suddenly too late and you can no longer

walk away. Jimmy was smoking in the lot, the rear lot

of the 7-Eleven, breaking down boxes, smoking, and as always,

at least on these nights I'd found myself walking in order to think,

as always he starts up with the insults, made to sound like flattery.

Tell me everything, he says, knowing there's nothing

to tell. Tell me, did you eat that pussy last night,
did you hit that pussy, did you hit it, he asks, knowing my eye
has already strayed from Alexis and there is no sex
to speak of, not for a couple weeks anyhow, but he passes me
the joint and I take it, into my lungs, and I know the night
is beginning. Jimmy works graveyard, he worked the graveyard
shift, high-school drop-out though he was close, so close
to an athlete scholarship at a D-2 school down south,
he took the graveyard shift instead. His family a good family,
not wealthy but not poor, blue collar, as my father might call it,
though Jimmy's collar was green, 7-Eleven green, the reddish-
orange logo over the heart, at least near it, he says he's sick
of bitches and why don't we drive out to the beach this weekend,
not the beach we normally go to, high school parties and bonfires,
but the beach over the border, in Massachusetts, no more bitches,
he says, or not these bitches anyway, get ourselves some pussy,
he says, holding in the smoke, deep in the lungs, then breathing
     out
a long plume into the cold night air, some new pussy.
Dirty language, son, dirty language, the voice behind us.
It's the preacher man. Oh snap, it's the preacher man, says Jimmy,
taking another toke, the preacher man, says Jimmy, like he's
some old friend, a late-night pal, expected to show up at this hour,
normal, a routine hang, out in the lot behind the lot,
Jimmy looks over at the Chinese restaurant, sloping down

maybe thirty-five to forty yards, its lights off except

for a rear light, security light, lighting up a few empty crates

and also, a little, the dumpster, but no cats are to be seen,

must be inside, says Jimmy, inside the dumpster, or inside

the restaurant, boiled and skinned and boned, wrapped in plastic

in the walk-in, General Tso's Cats, he says, laughing, get away

from these bitches, he says, some new pussy, he says, and you,

he says, looking me up and down, as if the preacher man

were no longer there, or was always there, why you started

      dressing

like a wigger, says Jimmy, I mean damn, tie your shoelaces,

and look at your hair, you got zeked, he says, zeked. Ezekiel,

says the preacher man, son of Buzzy, despised by the Jews,

may God strengthen him, says the preacher man, no son

of his own, no heir, his young wife dead, but then the cherubim,

four pinwheeling swords of flame, says the preacher man, and

      today

we have the bread, if nothing else, unto thee wheat, and barley,

and beans, and lentils and millet and spelt, Ezekiel, chapter four,

verse nine. The air had changed, and so had Jimmy's face.

I looked closely at the preacher man, the ragged sharkskin

jacket, the dark denim jeans, the muddy Timberlands,

and before it was suddenly too late to walk away

the preacher man walked away.

      Thus, the first incident.

I record it to leave nothing out. And yet, there was
a second incident, which is the incident they insisted
I recount in the office, the green light, the burgundy chair
empty and waiting to make its judgment. But to leave nothing out,
after the preacher man left, I followed him. Past the dumpster
behind the Chinese restaurant, a skunk skulking around
the bushes, the preacher man calling it by name, Smiley,
past Smiley the skunk and the lot behind the laundromat,
then a way, maybe seventy-five to eighty yards
past the laundromat until we, the preacher man and I, stopped,
near a heavy plastic tarp weighted with rocks on one end
and the other flap tied to a shopping cart filled with milk jugs
filled with water. I could hear the Mad River, flowing below
even in winter, even in the freezing cold the Mad River
flows. Only once, I remember, the surface glittered with ice.
He talked to me then, about school, my grades, if I had a girlfriend,
as if he were my father, or, rather, someone else's father,
a friend's father, making normal small talk. Then he turned to me,
took a seat on a log stump, and then situated another stump,
very smooth, very polished, almost like something purchased
at an art gallery, an antique shop, something my mother might
put in the den, just to have it there, the preacher man positioned
this other log in front of him, and before I could take a seat,
just assuming, I am embarrassed to say, assuming it was
for me, to sit and tell him about my grades, and karate,

and how I'd rather kiss Abby than Alexis, the preacher man

takes a fishing tackle box from under the tarp, opens it,

and places a spoon on the smooth top of the stump, takes a
    hammer

from the tarp and starts hammering on the spoon. He does this

for a minute or so, a steady hammering, but just thudding,

a bass line, nothing shrill, the hammer must have had a rubber
    head,

it must have been a mallet, like at the doctor's office, and each
    time

he hammers the spoon, at least the first few times, it jumps, a little,

like a knee, or, rather, the leg below the knee, a reflex,

a little jolt, and then after a minute or so he looks up

and says, Well, here you go. He hands me the spoon, and I have to
    walk

closer to him, still seated on his log, and I take the spoon,

now curled, curled in on itself: a ring. Try it out, he says,

and I know that means to try it on each finger until I find

the best finger, and I do, and it's my pointer finger,

or index finger, the more proper name. I delight in weakness,

he says, in insults, he says, in hardships, in persecutions,

in difficulties, for when I am weak, says the preacher man,

then I am strong. This part, said the sergeant, his knee brushing my
    knee,

leaning close, is this a direct transcript? Is this what the victim actually said? And I thought, before I spoke, victim, he called

the preacher man a victim, and yet, if he, the sergeant, had listened,

or had he ears to listen, as the preacher man might have said,

he would have known the preacher man was strong, in his

      weakness

he was strong and so he was no victim, despite what happened

after he gave me the spoon, the ring. What happened is that Jimmy

started laughing, Jimmy had followed us, had followed me

following the preacher man, twenty yards behind me, to guess,

and here he is saying isn't this the fucking best, how special,

is that like some sort of friendship ring, some sort of engagement

ring, you a couple fags now, what is this that I'm looking at?

Dirty language, says the preacher man, dirty language, son.

Jimmy approaches, gets close enough to blow smoke in my face,

if he still had his joint, but he doesn't, he doesn't blow smoke

in my face, his hands are empty, and so, now, is his face,

the way it looked at the end of the first incident, and now

in this moment I know this is the second incident,

and that these incidents are one, this night is the incident.

Spelt and barley and shit, spits Jimmy, toward the preacher man.

I can dig that. But tell me, he says, tell me why they gotta

force this hippie shit, this granola crap, on people, if I want

a Wendy's burger I'll have a Wendy's burger, if I choose

to eat my breakfast at work, a hot dog and Slurpee the end

of each shift, fifteen minutes with the door locked, a few minutes

to myself, some quiet, the only fucking time in my life
I get to think, then who says I need to eat lentils and barley
and twigs? But, by this time, the preacher man has already stowed
away his hammer and tackle box, his log stumps, sliding each
under the tarp, and he has begun to walk away, his Bible
in his right hand, his armpit, toward the brush and sparse winter
        trees
on the embankment, the ledge, overlooking the Mad River.
And we follow, though, this time, Jimmy follows the preacher man,
and I follow Jimmy.

        Jimmy has continued the discussion
about granola and flax and is yelling, arms stiff at his sides,
on the ledge, the edge of the precipice, and the preacher man
is no longer interested, no longer listening, it seems,
staring out, over the Mad River, maybe toward the next town,
the Still River, an illogical name for a river, impossible,
really, he seems to be staring beyond this town, this world,
and then Jimmy pokes him in the shoulder, from behind,
not rough but also not friendly, almost the way you might poke
a mannequin, uncanny in its likeness, so realistic,
or a wax figure in a museum, when no one is looking,
to see if it might move, even though you know it won't, it can't,
the preacher man will not budge, but he does say, to the water
below him, looking down, he says, Son. That's all. Son. Jimmy
        turns

the preacher man around, taking both shoulders, swiveling him
around, and says, I ain't no one's son, you crazy bum, and that's
when I lunge. Without thinking I lunge to punch Jimmy, to clock
him but I slip, in the mud, my shoes unlaced and tripping,
tripping forward, and my fist, the left one, though I am right-
      handed,
catches the preacher man in the temple, his left, to my right,
and though I barely graze him, the ring on my left hand grazes
his face, Jimmy steps forward and pushes him, the preacher man,
and he stumbles backward, tumbles, into the night.
                                       As I did,
out of my chair, the room no longer dimly lit but black,
then my eyes open, my father standing over me, his open hand,
his left, before him, my face burning as if held in ice water,
submerged, dunked, my father saying leave nothing out, nothing,
what about Jimmy, he's the one, my father says, my father
who had been standing in the doorway the whole time, now sitting
in the burgundy chair, his back rigid, saying Jimmy is the one
to blame, just say it, he struck the old man, he has nothing
to live for anyway, he's trash, just say it, but the sergeant
now has my father by both shoulders, the sergeant is telling him
to calm down, he is speaking both directly and calmly,
almost whispering, saying calm down, saying we'll take care of
      this.
The office is lit like a pumpkin, the sergeant's office, in his home,

I realize, at that moment, he'd taken me to his home, after
the incident, the second incident, after I'd pulled
the preacher man from the Mad River, carried him up the hill,
over my shoulder, I'm not sure how, after I get him up
the hill, over the embankment, Jimmy nowhere to be seen,
after I get him back under his tarp, with his logs and tackle
box, the preacher man's home, he now lying on his back,
I hear him, as I lie on my stomach, right beside him, breathing
now, steadily, just a bit of blood, beginning to cake,
at the temple, and above the eye, the preacher man says, Son,
go. And so I walk, the mile and a half to the police station,
trying to think, walking in order to think but nothing,
there is nothing there, I barely remember that walk, except
that once I get to the station, just as I open my mouth,
the sergeant takes a look at me and tells me to stop, he holds up
a hand and says stop, then takes me away, uncuffed, in a car
without sirens, without lights.
        You can lie down, on your stomach,
stretched out with your face in your hands, and stare out.
What would you see? If looking left to right, swiveling your head
slowly, like a coin-op camera for tourists, or these days a phone,
in this panorama you'd see houses, ordinary white houses,
and above, white steeples of the first Methodist church, then,
swiveling slowly, the VA clinic, houses, more houses, trees,
of course, spiny in winter, maples and oaks mostly, maybe a pine

or spruce here and there, the sky, of course, often gray, usually
gray but now suddenly blue, if you keep looking, looking harder
and deeper, the boarded-up KFC, off the interstate, bad location
but now they say it might become a medical marijuana operation,
or hospital, no one is sure, more houses, to the right past the
       highway,
swiveling, the new high school, the new football stadium,
then a family farm, been there generations, hogs and chickens,
a field of alfalfa, then the dam, built in 1955, after the hurricanes,
after the flood, they dammed up the Mad River, to keep us safe,
though some say the river is now a cesspool, unsafe, to drink from,
of course, but also to swim in, to wade in, though, if its name
is dramatic, ominous, the Mad River, even dammed
it is maybe five feet tall, or deep, I mean, where it runs through
town it is five feet at most, shorter than most men, full-grown men,
and even if it were shorter, or shallower, I mean, say
four feet, or three, or four inches even, three inches, a baby
can drown in that, they say, in an inch of water an infant
could drown, face-first, and that's how I found him, the preacher
       man,
in maybe six inches of water, the shallowest part
of the river, though, therefore, the most dangerous, to be face-
first in the rocks and trash, beer cans, twigs, broken glass,
and so when I pulled him by the shoulders, the chest,
trying to get him onto his back, when I finally got a good look

at him, his face, he was cut everywhere, it seemed, his face bloody,

blood in his nose, his eyes, his mouth, and so I took the sleeve

of my hoodie, the whole forearm of it, all I had, and wiped his face,

and wiped, until I saw he was only cut in one or two spots,

above an eye, the left, his right, and at his temple, his face looked

older, at least sixty, maybe sixty-five, someone eligible

for discounts at the movies, at restaurants, at grocery stores,

if he ever dared enter such a place, ask for such charity.

As he did today, after all these years, fourteen to be exact.

I was finishing up some paperwork in the office,

and was about to check on the new clerk to see if she'd changed

her register, her shift was over, but she'd begun the habit

of talking with the next cashier, a boy about her age, maybe

a little older, I'd seen it before and there was no harm

there, but of course I'm the manager, the night manager,

and if we're going to keep this business open all night

we need to keep things moving, keep things on schedule,

corporate says this is a trial run, we need to prove we can be

twenty-four-seven, in a town like this, the population

just enough to qualify, for corporate to take a chance,

we need to exceed all expectations, they like to say,

and there I am, on the wall, framed, Manager of the Month,

February, I try not to look but I do confess some pride,

a little, and so when the old man came up to me, from behind,

and poked me in the shoulder, I knew right away who it was.

He had seen my photo on the wall, and recognized me,

age thirty-one and already going bald, but he still crowned

with a full head of hair, silver as his jacket, but, of course,

it wasn't him. The preacher man had passed, yes, he'd died,

several years after the incident, and though there had been no
    wake,

no funeral, no witnesses to the death, just a dead man

under a tarp, which was left there a few days then taken down,

the Chinese restaurant buying the lot, opening another

Chinese restaurant, Chinese Garden #6, same menu

but only take-out, neon lights and nowhere to sit,

the preacher man was cremated and I offered,

to the puzzlement of the crematorium, their nonchalant

handing over of the box, not even an urn, I offered

to take it. I threw it on a winter's day into the river.

The sky was blue the next town over, where I'd done my time

at the juvie, six months, on the fourth floor overlooking

the Still River, then a year of community service,

I'd insisted on that, though my father and the sergeant

had kept their eyes on me in that dimly lit room I'd kept

my left hand in the pocket of my hoodie, as the preacher man

had advised, I had not let them know what my left hand had done.

I had thought that was the right thing to do, for Jimmy,

I mean, he was trash, as my father said, the whole town thought so,

and that is the kind of incident that could have defined him, his entire life, but not for someone like me, or so I had thought,

and so I did my time, I had insisted, and Jimmy went off

to college, after all, I have heard, and here I am, walking in order

not to think, late at night, early in the morning, aisle #9.

The old man comes up from behind, and if he reaches out

because he feels something, something radiating from me,

or if he only wants to find some simple item for his home,

a picture frame or garden hose, I do not know, I will never know,

for the night clerk, the one who needs to change her register,

the one I have sometimes imagined as a daughter, or even

someday, a wife, I confess, has already come between us.

She must have looked up, while chatting with the boy,

at her register, #5, starting to get her bills and receipts in order,

her silver and copper coins rolled, she must have looked up

and seen me, standing alone, 3:55 a.m., aisle #9, a hammer

in my hand, with a rubber head, what's called a mallet,

and, even from that distance, saw that I was overcome.

Portrait of My Father as John Clare: "To an Infant Daughter"

Fresh-cut pumpkin stem,
two bushel of fiddleheads,
pinch of crushed chokecherry
seed, eye of 'possum, bitter
root of sassafras sapling threshed
from the turnpike shoulder
(it's where they like to grow),
boiled in a drum of Housatonic
River water twenty-four hours,
stirred with sugarcane six feet tall,
and finally, drunk, for breakfast,
a gypsy recipe your grandmother
scrawled down after my long
sterile year of marriage. I doubt
your mother ever saw me drink it,
but she must've smelled it, wondered
what new bad idea I was cooking
up for money. O life is but a drug
you keep buying, borrowing
to buy, even though the high
faded the day your father woke
the house with a bellows full
of angry wind, a fireplace
on fire, ancestral photos
melting on the mantel. My father.
Who thought, but did not say,
this bitch I married is a half-Indian,
half-Scottish witch. Saw it behind
his eyes. I did. The wish to drift
and perish. My daughter, let your ears
open like rain opens the marsh
to primordial chants of bullfrogs,

horseflies swarming the ceremony,
the storm stampeding the pond.
Then maybe pray for your father,
who once stood at the edge of traffic
(it's where he liked to go) and cut you
vein by vein by vein from the earth.

Portrait of My Father as John Clare: "Epithalamion"

And how, when she must've thought I was asleep,
she loved herself with a candlestick, then slipped
it back inside her bedside drawer. Next morning,
she cooking biscuits in lard, I snuck myself
a whiff: cattail soaked in rainwater
off a tin roof, the slightest tang of sorghum.
I've pictured it many times, that dark system
that gives life, recoils, beckons, the whole thing
cupped in the palm of a hand, if one
so dared. But when I bring my hands together
over my wife, my sleeping wife, they slide
away, one north, one southwest, and I'm left
looking like a man in the middle of traffic,
stripped clean of his vesture, directing no one.

Photograph of My Parents Exchanging Vows

Of course they're not smiling
because this is serious—
the delicate slipping

of ring onto her finger,
hidden under his hand, still
fair-skinned, almost hairless.

The left half of the Bible
eclipsing the hem
of white, gauzy veil.

1970s-blue eyeshadow
and tarantula mascara.
A stray frosted curl.

Handlebar moustache
and clipped muttonchops.
A single laugh line.

Her pug nose, my thin lips;
his dimpled chin, my sunken eyes.
Their framed proximity.

And if you stare long
enough, it seems
she almost squints

as his knuckles begin
to tighten and raise
into something like a promise.

But it's months before
he'll do that to her.
This isn't about that.

The Good Life

Learn yourself a trade. Plumbing, carpentry, electrical work, butchering, doesn't matter. That's what my father said. Learn yourself a trade then get a job. 9-5, 8-5, 7-3, 7-5, don't matter. Take the hours, as many as they'll give you. The hours aren't for you. They're for your wife and kids. Of course, he said, find yourself a wife. Not these harlots in the colleges. Good girl, girl you meet at church, girl who makes her own apple butter, knits little caps to keep the kids warm in winter. Pay your gas bill. Pay your electric bill. If you have a chimney and fireplace, chop your own wood. Shovel your own snow. You're making enough money to hire a kid to shovel your snow, you're making too much money. Give it to the church. Give it to the bums. You got extra give it to a man who will shine your shoes on a box he made by hand. Polish your work boots. Carry a briefcase. Man don't need a hoity-toity job to carry a briefcase. Put your tools in it, your lunch. Other guys at the plant make fun, let them. Carry a briefcase and give anything extra to the shoeshiners and the bums. Jesus Christ was a bum. Don't mind me saying. A wandering holy bum, with no wife, no kids. Some say he had a harlot, but they had no colleges back then. Back then a man learned on his own. How to live the good life. A trade, a wife and kids, biscuits and homemade apple butter, and unless you were the son of God himself, only as much snow as you could shovel.

Portrait of My Father as John Clare: "Skunk's Nest"

Well in my many walks I rarely found
a place less likely for a skunk to make
its nest—or bed—or home—than a dumpster
in the parking lot of the Westport cab stand,
where on so many nights I'd tossed the news.
Now little Smiley—it's what I've named him—
keeps warm among those tattered inky pages,
styrofoam cups, shredded lottery tickets,
diapers, disposable cell phones. Slept there
myself one night, or should say, tried to sleep.
In the woods, I'd found my car burned: some kids
probably, bored or stoned, and so I salvaged
what I could, couple handfuls of nickels
and dimes, the tire iron, a few pine cones
I could now use like charcoal, to sketch
fairer scenes than this. And as the snow
came down slow and pond'rous
I traversed paths named and unnamed and,
when nearly blind, stumbled upon the dumpster.
Quiet. So quiet and dark. Like being in a skull
inside a skull. Like that. Now, listen: Smiley
has a nose like a grape. The purple kind. And I know
that means he will not last the night. I feed him
McDonald's burgers but he only eats the bread.
I once ate grass along an old ditch road,
and it tasted like dough. Now when I eat bread
I taste fields, sunlight. The dog I used to chase
and let chase me was named Smiley. When bit
by a 'possum Ma put him down. He made
one noise. She said go out and find the wretched
animal and kill it with the same clam rake
she used on Smiley. I searched for it two days

and two nights, or pretended to. Finally found
a raccoon dead from cold at the edge of the road,
tied it inside a plastic bag. Ma said damn
me for bringing it inside the house, wasn't her
who taught me to be so stupid, go bury
the thing outside. I carried the raccoon down
the old dump road and kept walking. Hours
later, found myself at the edge of the marsh,
at the factory where they make helicopter wings—
or talons—or blades. In the sky, nothing
but a few gulls, a robin. I threw the animal
in a dumpster. The noise it makes? A church bell,
if you are hidden inside the bell, praying.

Hood

He'd have drowned, without me.
The eyes underwater green,
gray, shut. Without a word I

struck him, then, the second time
and the rest said what, probably,
he expected: *bum, psycho, scum.*

On the ground his Bible, torn
tissue bookmarking its final pages.
Words, fists, failed—so I dragged

him down to the Mad River
and pushed him in. If between
sight and seen, blood and bled,

there is a bridge like trust,
I would not be the one
to ask: *hood, punk, druggie,*

scum. Ask me for some spare
change, ask me if I pray (no,
and no), but do not ask me

to save your life: between what
the water says and what it does,
I am already here, shouldering you.

Portrait of My Father as John Clare: "Warbler's Nest"

O thunder you rupture
the trunk, the husk, the mask,
but behind the eyes lives

a creature so utterly devout
to its nest it will expel
its own defect—long-

legged hobbler, blind
pair of wings—and watch
the little orphan drop

between the mossy crevices
of roots and stones, the funeral
homes for strangled singers.

Portrait of My Father as John Clare: "Coon Cat's Nest"

Can one become a coon cat?
Or must one be born designed
with ears as big as poplar
leaves and whiskers long enough
to call a beard? Take this coon
in my car trunk, for instance:
on a wet day like today
she must weigh my tackle box
plus at least one of my steel-
toed boots. She's sleeping now, tired
from being chased by hoodlum
boys who escape the suburbs
to cause some forest bedlam
with sticks and stones, cigarette
lighters set to gas-soaked rags
held underneath a hobo's
home, his car he no longer
drives so shelters with plastic
tarp, embellishes with twigs
and ferns and milkweed he picked
in June. But July showers
sucker-punched with sudden
gusts and the tarp flew up
like a swift from a chimney
choked with smoke. I climbed an oak
and tore it down, then stayed still
as the hoodlums' liquor-laced
hooting made their purpose known.
I watched the fire from above.
Can one become a bigger
man? I ask the coon awake
from nap, the trunk lid open

halfway for air and a slice
of moon. But she does not say.
Her grayish-white fur appears
streaked with black, not natural
marking but a charcoal smudge
from something burnt: newspapers
or hot dog buns or a bag
of laundry I'd meant to clean
down by the river. The creek,
I mean, it's not much wider
than a rib cage, though it runs
all night even as you sleep.

Another Story About the Body

The child keeps screaming in its highchair. The mother has examined its fingers, its fingernails, just beginning to form into something that can be called nails, the lips, mouth, tongue, back of the tongue, pink nub of tonsil, the child's breath split pea soup and infant rage, or fear, the father thinks it's fear, has looked around the kitchen for any sign of danger, black cat under the table, bear in the window, boogeyman peek-a-booing from the pantry, but there's nothing but the half-empty cupboards, the mostly empty refrigerator, the paint-peeled window frame looking out not onto some fairy tale wilderness but a city, deindustrialized, 1977, where a man can have his hours on the docks cut in half, can have his ear grazed by an eighty-pound iron hook as he hoists another box of freight and still, still the child screams, the mother's fingers are under the child's armpits, as if to make it laugh, are in the crooks of its elbows, its knees, her fingers coming up empty, the infant's mouth an O of O make it stop, O mommy, O daddy, but the baby can only scream a scream until, finally, the noise stops, the mouth still open, the eyes still open and wet and white as if blind. The mother begins to cry. What is it? she says. The father, by the open window, turns, and in his son's left ear he sees it: a single yellowjacket. And before he restores their three lives to one, he covets that bee, which, now dead, quiets half the world with its unbuzzing.

Portrait of My Father as John Clare: "[Prose Sketch]"

Fair meadows and hollows leveled by grass what they call greens mowed smooth as algae on shale for a rich man's sport and concrete boxes selling TVs longer than bathtubs and phones that snap photos of nothing where bonnie Rosemary and her sisters they did run and wires thick as wrists stretch over every view of sun and cloud and tree branch whether white and pink with blossom or winter-stripped and lakes cradled not by God's packed earth but rather some plastic engineered to feel sickly like skin and where few fish swim except trout who belong in rivers so men can pay to put on rubber britches and wade into some imaginary land it makes me melancholy and wretched—on the contrary a creek though clogged with broken beer bottles and fast food wrappers Wendy's Arby's and Burger King and condoms slick and broken makes me feel hidden and free under the bough of twigs and brush not quite trees but stretched out above maybe like swords at funerals for soldiers or arms of family and loved ones at a wedding as the bride and groom dash beneath laughing and ruddy and splashed with champagne a cheerful accident and how good to take off your boots with beloved Rosemary out here alone years later the rustling creek overshadowed perhaps with cloud as if the sky's dome thickens like pesky old thoughts and threatens to burst—these scenes though I am nearly gone I say make me happy as if I were in Paradise but maybe later the earth's first few years and decades perhaps most when the flood did come and few deserved even a twig to hold onto.

To Egon Schiele, 1912,
After His Imprisonment

You kept traveling. Through Bregenz, Bodolz, places you had seen as a boy. You painted boats and castles, sunflowers. You could not, of course, return to Neulengbach, where your landlord held for ransom some of your paintings. The proof of your insolence had already been presented in court; you sat still as the judge ceremoniously torched one of your portraits. But not of Tatjana Georgette Anna von Mossig.

It must have been a sketch, one of hundreds, of a woman, crouched or kneeling semi-nude, or lying on her back, shoes laced and garters tied with ribbon, her legs spread, touching herself.

You never touched her—not Tatjana. The daughter of a naval officer, she had followed you home for weeks. And you did not let her in. She must have loved you, as a child loves a stranger, an artist in a town of mothers and fathers and churches.

The police found her sleeping under your window. Twenty-four days of your twenty-fourth year you spent in jail for the sketches and paintings in your studio, which they must have touched, and held, for evidence.

Here, at Lake Constance, in silent Bohemia, you stop. You look across the water, this pause in the Rhine that separates you from Switzerland, the Alps glittering like purple quartz. You write, *I long for a free people. I want to begin a new life.* And you paint this chestnut tree. It is young; its red trunk is thinner than the stake it is tied to; its leaves are green and few. Maybe someone, having escaped the war, and the Spanish flu, which will kill more than the war, including you, your mother, and the respectable woman you will convince yourself to marry, will one morning untie this tree and cut its fruit.

I would have touched her, Egon. On the shoulder, and on the neck. I would have taken her from Neulengbach and brought her here, and painted this tree. And given her paper and pencil and said now you, *now it's your turn.* And: another, draw another. And another. I would have traveled along the edge of the river with Tatjana Georgette Anna von Mossig and each day stopped with her to lunch. And spread her trees on the grass and looked at them.

And, when it is dark, and she is ready: the flare of paper, of stem and leaf, each vein licked along its length by smoke, a slow slide of limbs, locked and twisted in shadow—the first of our nightly lessons in burning.

Inis Oírr

Oh, must we dream our dreams
and have them, too?
              -Elizabeth Bishop

I had wanted to see it
to see it. It was in our book.
And look: just over this rock
piled upon rock, a crooked mast,
and another, shorter—orange? russet?

You had wanted to go back.
It was cold. The jagged, limestone
maze of this place cast a waning spell
in the rain and fog and wind.
We'd already seen the Holy Well of St. Enda;
grazed with our hands the gutted insides
of a topless church—above us every size
and century of grave and Celtic cross,
the sky; we'd done two of the three pubs;
the lighthouse; the dock; and, of course, atop the island,
O'Brien's Castle, Cromwell-gouged
but sturdy, a proto-Martello overlooking
the living: a horse hauling a hen party,
a drowsy couple of boot-licking donkeys,
black-faced sheep ripe for shearing, cows
upon cows, the soaked shepherd barking
at the sea, even a camera-shy cormorant,
out-of-season and corner-of-the-eye,
but a cormorant, not a heron or egret,
we agreed. If that wasn't enough, outside
our bed-and-breakfast, an old geezer
of a plant blooming bloody cranesbill,
my favorite flower.

I wanted to see it. I took you by the hand,
and we hiked the last dung-coated stretch
of road, hugging the coast—but no, the masts
were gone. Below (we now looked down
from some sort of grassy precipice), a lake,
three dozen or so swans, and across the gap,
through the haze, the five villages, clustered
like an American city seen from a plane,
but feeling farther away ...

It was there, behind us, hidden on the other side
of the bluff, or steep, or crag, whatever it was.
The shipwreck, the whole rusty hulk of it
balanced high above tide, precariously,
for decades. Not one crewman had drowned;
every one of them rescued, so said our book.
Torn on a reef, the sunken ship had lain
submerged, out of sight, until the Atlantic
threw it back. Imagine: the wet beast
battered, barnacled, bandaged with kelp
and carrageen, its two crooked masts alert
to the breeze. Imagine the first villager
to wake at dawn, a little hung-over, maybe,
on mulled honey wine. Beside him, his wife
of seven days, a wool sweater wrapped
around her shoulders. How he leads her
down the hill, for a bit of air, and then
the unbelievable vision, impossibly
dripping, heaving, flushed with brine,
as if he himself had put it there
with his own hands, and wants to show her.

Feral

We name the new feral "Tomatillo," after the color of her eyes. Despite her lithe, Greyhound-like frame, she is just a kitten. During her first feeding, dry food from my hand, her nose wet like the grass we sit in, she suddenly gallops toward a grasshopper, maybe a bumblebee. My father once told me bumblebees don't sting, which is not true, at least for me on the day we hiked along the Housatonic River, grilling hot dogs over twigs, throwing a knife over and over into a tree. I remember my thumb swelling like a grape, green with poison, the pain coming only after, when my father told me what had happened. Already, I love this cat. And Bodega and Luce, our older ferals—almost as much as our two indoor cats. My wife says Tomatillo has a better shot outside, sleeping under the abandoned house behind ours, than in a shelter. *They'd kill it,* she says. Too many cats. *An American dilemma,* I say. *A Japanese dilemma, too,* she says, sipping decaf. She is pregnant with our first child. *A whole island of cats,* she says, *a feral kingdom in the Pacific.* A national nuisance, quarantined. But, I don't say, why love a thing less when there is more of it? Why find it less beautiful? This summer, as an experiment, we have let our backyard bloom into wildness. Grass, weeds, flowers, bushes, garden, an abundance uncut. In the mornings, in slippers and flannel, with a bag of kibble, I stand in the cold mountain air and look. I breathe it in. Then—when it moves—I wade, up to my calves, my thighs, my waist, my ribs, and I bend searching for the bowls.

Portrait of My Father as John Clare: "Common Loon's Nest"

I think of ma stretched out like death
in Room 42 of the Pequot Motel,
the television static rain,
not snow, as they say, the whole room soaked
through like a rag before it's squeezed.
I'd left the faucet on, indeed, a quick shave
before work, my twelve-hour shift
driving a cab—then coming home after fries
and a Double Whopper with cheese
in a parking lot lit up like some firefly
graveyard, wing dust on my windshield,
stardust in my head. And that's what they called it,
trying to be kind, perhaps, doctors
and nurses, not in white suits but suits with neckties,
flowered dresses and scarves of gold.
Stardust—as if I were Brando
or Paul Newman rocking away his last days
at the Connecticut General Hospital
for the Insane. Yes, quite a name
for a place serving pot roast with plastic knives,
pressing hot towels to faces
of tenants not allowed to shave themselves. Ma
told me to not forget her soup
and crackers, Meals on Wheels had lately been stale
as my jokes. I wiped the bloody
foam from my face, made sure the TV was set
to channel 9, PBS, left
without saying goodbye. As I did tonight,
though we have no TVs, only
the large one like some aquarium lighting
up the lounge. The other men stare
and moan night and day as if it's God Himself,

as if God played golf or dropped bombs
on hospitals in ancient lands
still here, its people wailing for their newborn
dead, a sound I carry with me
everywhere, even here, this pond I've named
Hidden Loon Pond, whether it's my right to name
God's pond or not. I am Adam
as much as Eve, though, it took me my whole life
to figure that one out. Listen:
the loon, what's called the common loon, yodeling
across the pond. They make their nests
with marsh grass and sedge, in the coves
and dark bays of the pond, if it's big enough.
I once saw a loon in the lot
of Circuit City after a heavy storm.
It must have mistaken the slick
asphalt for pond, the neon glare for moonlight.
It took nearly twenty minutes
to find enough runway, like a propeller
plane before, finally, it levels
its wings and lifts from the ground. The common loon
is named for its hobble, from the Swedish word
for *lame*. I myself can barely
walk a mile and, worse, tonight when I escaped
that prison I forgot my shoes.
Yes, prison, that's what I called it, the first room
I could have stayed in forever,
no rent, no hollering ma, and as much food
as an idle man can eat. Now
look at me: sitting barefoot by the cattails
of this marshy pond, listening
for the common loon, hiding, which is the sane
thing to do in this whirlipuff
of a world. Some of us, like the brown mallard,
can only fly against the wind.
Most of us can't fly at all, and so we turn
away, pray for a mighty gust.

Late Twentieth Century in the Form of Litany

The box spring smoldered in the dumpster the first time I died.
My father tore tissue into tissue tiny as drops of blood the first
    time I died.
I pushed the movie theater's back metal door out into the sunlight
    the first time I died.

There was the hissing mouth of the Canada Goose inches from
    mine the first time I died.
There was the marsh of cattails and rain, gnats and horseflies and
    mist the first time I died.
A bucket of bluefish—baby snappers—drowning on the warped
    wooden dock the first time I died.

I wanted to say he can't hurt us now the first time I died.
I helped her roll pink plastic tubes into her long bleached hair the
    first time I died.
Her eyes less brown than brown with flecks of green and amber
    and cheap clover honey if you look really close right
    before the first time you die.

She wanted to say he's far, far away the first time we died.
In the summer the box fan melted on the windowsill until we died.
In the winter the gas man came and we had no money and hid in
    the closet and she lit another cigarette and blew the smoke
    through the slats in the door until he died.

We slept in the car with the motor running and the heat at full blast
    the first time she died.
She took her kids to the eighteenth floor of the housing project
    where another nurse's aide lived and where he'd never
    think to look for us and she died.
She opened the oven door before sunrise and we sat before it
    rubbing our hands near the blue flickering flame until it
    died.

Neil Sedaka on eight-track tape the first time I died.
Neil Diamond on eight-track tape the first time I died.
We slept in the car and she lit a cigarette and thunder only happens
    when it's raining because no one admits it when they're
    only pretending to sleep.

I ate Reese's Pieces and a boy and his alien flew on a bike across
    the moon the first time I died.
I ate Charlie Chans and watched a man run and run on the beach
    toward Paris, France, or maybe it was Jerusalem, the first
    time I died.
She held my hand in the dark and a man named Rambo oiled his
    gun like each muscle of his body the first time I died.

My father picked me up in a car he called a Gremlin the first time I
    died.
My father pulled up slow in a small limousine and I wondered
    why we never see baby pigeons the first time I died.
The judge revoked custody is what I heard her say and I wondered
    if he could fit a small flock of Canada Geese in his
    limousine or if they would die.

Ronald Reagan shot in the armpit the first time he died.
Travis Bickle mohawked and mugging for the mirror the first time
    he died.
Mark David Chapman caressing the signature on John and Yoko's
    Double Fantasy and why did rat poison look like candy?

It was a hearse not a limousine my mother told me and she didn't
    know where he got such crazy ideas.
She didn't know the story of the boy who hid in the coat rack at
    Sears and who was beaten for nineteen minutes until
    someone called the police.
She didn't know and then she did

                              and when my father died
years later, he refused: the chemo, the radiation, the nurse, the

doctors, the orderlies, the turkey and peas, the white walls
and white curtains,
and his brother, I have heard, massaged his feet and read dog-
eared passages of scripture on sheets of paper thin as my
father's eyelids.

I didn't see it coming, the gray waves of the Atlantic rushing
toward me, inside me, the undertow, then after blackness
my father's proud arms around his boy who he had just
taught to swim, even if it nearly killed him.
The first time I died I looked out from the tower at my city
beneath me and could swear there was no way it could
nearly fit inside both my palms.
When I died I heard your cry, I swear I did, my child, and I went
to the windows of whatever we were lucky enough to
dwell inside, and opened them, one at a time, and waited
for the light that comes slowly, more slowly than we have
been told, but comes.

There Will Be a Future

There will be red lentils and cauliflower
on a small chipped plate. Steamed milk
and coffee on the stove and your finger
licking the froth from your father's beard.
There will be fresh-cut penstemen
in a mason jar beside the whiskey.
Books. So many books. Chipped Buddha
and Mary in her red candle keeping watch
as a cat tortures a cricket on the carpet.
As mother hammers another vista
into the wall. There will be a future.
While you, my daughter, look down
from this mountain at other mountains
on fire, know there will be water
to search for. There will be singing
about the water. The fires. Ponderosa
pine and the bark beetles that devour
their veins. Ravens. So many ravens. Smoke
rising from bread over an open fire.

Notes

"Prayer (After Refusing to Pray)" takes its title from Patrick Donnelly's poem "Prayer After Refusing to Pray," from the book *The Charge*.

"Oración por Tim Cook" is for Tim Cook, the author's friend (not the CEO of Apple).

"St. Patrick's Day, Chicago": the line "Broken river, you're not broken after all" is taken from Dean Young's poem "Another Strange Rose for the Afterlife," from the book *Fall Higher*.

"Three Rivers" is in memory of Sayaka Kanade.

"Mad River" and "Hood": the sentence "He'd have drowned, without me" is taken from the opening line of Carl Phillips's poem "Shimmer," from the book *Silverchest*. In its formal obsessiveness and peripatetic fever, "Mad River" also owes a debt to the novella *Walking* by Thomas Bernhard (translated by Kenneth J. Northcott). Also, the lines "Do not walk away/ early enough and it is suddenly too late and you can no longer / walk away" are adapted from the following in Bernhard's novella: "If you do not walk away early enough, said Kerrer, it is suddenly too late and you can no longer walk away."

The interspersed sequence of poems "Portraits of My Father as John Clare" draws inspiration from the British Romantic poet John Clare (1793-1864).

"Portrait of My Father as John Clare: 'To an Infant Daughter'": the phrase "a bellows full of angry wind" is taken from W.B. Yeats's poem "A Prayer for My Daughter," from the book *Michael Robartes and the Dancer*.

"The Good Life" takes its title from the poem by Jon Davis, in the book *Preliminary Report.*

"Another Story About the Body" takes its title from the poem "A Story About the Body" by Robert Hass, in the book *Human Wishes.*

"To Egon Schiele, 1912, After His Imprisonment" is addressed to the Austrian artist Egon Schiele (1890-1918).

"Feral" is for Erin.

"Late Twentieth Century in the Form of Litany" takes its title from the poem by Gabrielle Calvocoressi, in the book *Apocalyptic Swing.* The author's poem—as does Calvocoressi's—pays homage to the poem "My Twentieth Century" by Tom Andrews, in the book *Random Symmetries.*

"There Will Be a Future" is for Thalia. The poem takes its title from the poem by Adam Zagajewski, in the book *Tremor* (translated by Renata Gorczynski).

Acknowledgements

The author wishes to thank the editors of the following magazines, who published these poems, sometimes in earlier versions:

Agenda (U.K.): "To Egon Schiele, 1912, After His Imprisonment"

The Collagist: "Oración por Tim Cook"

Diode: "The Good Life," "Another Story About the Body," "Feral"

Driftless Review: "Three Rooftops"

Forklift, Ohio: "Patron Saint," "Portrait of My Father as John Clare: 'Common Loon's Nest'," "Portrait of My Father as John Clare: 'Coon Cat's Nest'"

Four Way Review: "The Superintendent"

The Gettysburg Review: "Photograph of My Parents Exchanging Vows," "Inis Oírr"

Indiana Review: "My Father's Car"

iO: "Twenty Thousand Pigeons," "St. Patrick's Day, Chicago"

The Minnesota Review: "Photograph of My Stepfather with Handguns"

New England Review: "Prayer (After Refusing to Pray)" (as "Prayer After Refusing to Pray"), "Three Rivers"

North Dakota Quarterly: "Portrait of My Father as John Clare: 'Skunk's Nest'," "Portrait of My Father as John Clare: 'Epithalamion'"

Ploughshares: "Empire," "Fassbinder"

RHINO: "Portrait of My Father as John Clare: 'To an Infant Daughter'"

Tinderbox Poetry Journal: "Mad River" (as "Midnight Peripatetic")

Tupelo Quarterly: "Late Twentieth Century in the Form of Litany"

A number of these poems first appeared in the chapbook *Twenty Thousand Pigeons* (iO, 2014).

"Oración por Tim Cook" and "Three Rivers" were republished in *The Narrow Chimney Reader, Vol. 1* (Uptown Pubhouse Press, 2015).

*

Much gratitude to Diane Seuss and Candice Amich for their insights and care for this book in its last stages. Thanks to those who have helped to shape and encourage this book along the way: Martha Rhodes, Alan Williamson, Reginald Gibbons, Brooks Haxton, Gabrielle Calvocoressi, C. Dale Young, Matthew Olzmann, Vievee Francis, Matt Hart, Dahlia Porter, Tim Cook, Jynne Dilling Martin, Melanie Ross, Nestor Ramos, Dave Peterson, Courtney Craggett, Kara Candito, and Rebecca Gayle Howell.

Thank you, Kyle McCord and Nick Courtright, for believing in this book, for your essential editorial vision, and for being such bad asses.

Respect to Jim Daniels, my first poetry teacher and still my model for what it means to be a poet.

My extended Warren Wilson MFA community: thank you.

Admiration and thanks to my dear friends and colleagues in the Creative Writing program at Northern Arizona University: Nicole Walker, Lawrence Lenhart, Andie Francis, Ann Cummins, Jane Armstrong, Bo Schwabacher, and Erin Stalcup.

Giraffe hugs to my *Waxwing* family: Erin Stalcup, Todd Kaneko, Curtis Bauer, Dexter Booth, Jenny Johnson, Grace Liew, Toni Jensen, Candice Amich, Anna Clark, Corey Campbell, Rajiv Mohabir, Grace Fenlason, Lauren Kalt, Jason Robinson, and Nick Fox.

Love to my family, in particular those who've helped raise me up: Rosemary Sandor, Robert Bigos, George Sandor, Velma Byman, Selina Bigos, Janet Stalcup, and Thomas Stalcup.

My beating heart, Erin and Thalia: you sustain and increase me.

About Gold Wake Press

Gold Wake Press, an independent publisher, is curated by Nick Courtright and Kyle McCord. All Gold Wake titles are available at amazon.com, barnesandnoble.com, and via order from your local bookstore. Learn more at goldwake.com.

Available Titles:

Eileen G'Sell's *American Radiance*
Glenn Shaheen's *Carnivalia*
Frances Cannon's *The High and Lows of Shapeshift Ma and Big-Little Frank*
Erin Stalcup's *Every Living Species*
Kelly Magee's *The Neighborhood*
Kyle Flak's *I Am Sorry for Everything in the Whole Entire Universe*
David Wojciechowski's *Dreams I Never Told You & Letters I Never Sent*
Keith Montesano's *Housefire Elegies*
Mary Quade's *Local Extinctions*
Adam Crittenden's *Blood Eagle*
Lesley Jenike's *Holy Island*
Mary Buchinger Bodwell's *Aerialist*
Becca J. R. Lachman's *Other Acreage*
Joshua Butts' *New to the Lost Coast*
Tasha Cotter's *Some Churches*
Hannah Stephenson's *In the Kettle, the Shriek*
Nick Courtright's *Let There Be Light*
Kyle McCord's *You Are Indeed an Elk, but This Is Not the Forest You Were Born to Graze*
Kathleen Rooney's *Robinson Alone*
Erin Elizabeth Smith's *The Naming of Strays*

About Justin Bigos

Justin Bigos is the author of a previous collection of poems, the chapbook *Twenty Thousand Pigeons* (iO, 2014). His writing has appeared in publications including *Ploughshares*, *New England Review*, *Indiana Review*, *Forklift Ohio*, *McSweeney's Quarterly*, and *The Best American Short Stories 2015*. He cofounded and coedits the literary journal *Waxwing* and makes his home in Flagstaff, Arizona, where he teaches at Northern Arizona University.

CPSIA information can be obtained
at www.ICGtesting.com
Printed in the USA
FFOW03n1258200218
45193808-45721FF